A Map to Find Each Other

A Map to Find Each Other

Poems by

Janet Jerve

Cover design by Shay Culligan
Cover art by Maarja Roth

ISBN: 978-1-63980-144-2

Kelsay Books
502 South 1040 East, A-119
American Fork, Utah 84003
Kelsaybooks.com

for my husband Rod and the animals
that brought us closer to the natural world

Acknowledgments

The following poems have appeared in print:

Poetry East: "Fortune" and "Moon or Star"

Amethyst and Agates: Poems of Lake Superior (Holy Cow! Press):
"Speaking to Lake Superior Elders"

Contents

Preface

2020 was a rare and frightening year. By March, everyone felt an invisible wave of fear sweeping around the globe as the spread of an unknown virus became a pandemic. Families were sequestered in their homes, schools closed, and people worked from home. Few people traveled. Airports and freeways were empty. Besides the birds singing and dogs barking in people's yards, it was silent, more like living up north in the wilderness. The worldwide fear was palpable and shifted how everyone lived.

For my husband Rod and me, the fear, anxiety, silence, and isolation enveloping the world had been our reality for the prior two years. Three weeks into retirement, Rod lost the ability to walk and became a wheelchair user due to a previously undetected congenital spinal defect. Rod had round-the-clock nursing care; the transition home was difficult because he was worried about me caring for him all alone. To survive this life change, we had to learn how to stay focused on the moment and zero in on each task at hand. If I let myself look back in regret or project into the future, I could not have peace of mind.

Mobility for Rod was difficult, and travel was no longer possible for us. We learned to appreciate the simplicity of life. We laughed every day and began watching comedians before we went to bed. To stay healthy and strong, I exercised by walking, riding my bike, hiking, and skiing. Writing, however, did not come easily, and to attempt to coax the muse, I gave myself an assignment: when I was out in nature if I saw an animal, I had to write about it.

When Covid came, all at once, our limited way of living became the norm. We were experienced in facing fear and dealing with it. We embraced creativity. Rod ordered supplies and built his workshop in the basement. I ordered wallpaper and paint and channeled my late mother to help me remember how to hang wallpaper. Poems again came quickly to me, and they were healing and a joy to write. This book chronicles the past four years and the animals that accompanied us on our journey.

Ours is the world of the swallow wing,
a scene turning and curving, and we are
in it, scribing our own reflection of heaven.
—William Stafford

Sacred

I used to lie across the picnic table
watching clouds drift while birds
sang out of sight in the woods.
They were just background sound.
Why didn't I let them in deeper,
feel a shiver in my skin?
I remember my mother's interest in birds,
the smell of food cooking, friends
climbing the back hill asking me to come with them.
If I listened back then, I thought of it
as killing time while I waited to play.
Before I knew it, life shifted to a long workday.
Now I want to stay home, listen to
the birds in the backyard, an important task
I let slip years ago. I want to hear them,
sing songs that were lost to the wind,
hear what seeps through closed windows
on days too cool to open the house to birdsong.
They are primary now, sacred.

Turtle

Twice in one hike
along the Hyland trail
I see a turtle.

Both times
someone picks her up.
Her legs swim,

her neck cranes
until she's set off-trail
and into the brush.

That's me—tucked
into my shell, waiting
to be set aright.

I have been
on this path
a long time

and have come
to a crossroads
before.

Still, I don't
always know
which way to go.

Promise

You hike with your friends and
as they forge on with fervor
you note tingling in your arm,

remember the promise to self,
to the doctor: stop when
you feel numbness or pain.

But you don't stop, as if to stop
will mean you will lose them all—
your friends, all the unmet promises

you hang onto for yourself
and others—and you keep going,
knowing it is past time to stop.

When you finally call out
that you are heading back,
you turn to see them weave

through the woods and beyond,
and you take your own path
to circle back to your car.

A sudden crash on the right triggers alarm
as limbs crack, underbrush and bramble break
in a succession of spills, tumbling down the hill.

Silence, a sprinkling of green,
brown on brown, tan on tan, and stillness.
Then him, standing there looking at you—

a yearling with the fuzz and muster
of stumpy antlers stands only feet away,
looking at you wide-eyed and you at him.

You flush, and blood pumps to distant cells,
healing you. Deer stand for gentleness
and kindness, kindness from the universe.

In a Wash of Sunlight

Rooted in the garden of despair,
I scatter seeds of solemn
laments all over the yard.

Someone will need to come soon
to clear darkness from light.

It isn't until I face east and lean north
that I allow myself to be pulled by the roots,
become free enough to move freely

out of the sun's glare and into the
centeredness of shade and stare at the
wild geraniums growing in my yard.

Here, have them, she said.
I pull them like weeds from my garden.
Planted last year, the geraniums thrive.

Flat feathered leaf, tiny purple flower—
they are beautiful, yet common, simple.
Completely free, they didn't cost a dime.

Locked in my gaze, I first hear thudding vibration,
then see a brilliant iridescent hummingbird
taking center stage in a wash of sunlight

to hover over the tiniest of purple flowers,
dip its beak down into the petaled goblet,
and shimmer with joy.

Nothing Left Unsaid

Spinal cord cancer took him from the life he imagined
at retirement. He was never one to have a long bucket list
to check off before dying, but he did want more of what
he already loved: hiking, biking, and skiing.

We left our beloved neighborhood—the lake
across the street, the heron standing guard to welcome
the rising and setting sun—for one-level-living
better suited to a wheelchair, and though we found

a lovely new home, the list of losses piled one upon
another and became overwhelming. My tall, broad-shouldered
husband, was now shorter than me in his wheelchair.
Chores, once equally shared, fell unto my shoulders

and were hauntingly short-listed for him. Loss ate away
at everything he stood for: pride in hard work,
being the husband who never expected to be served,
the father who fed his children first, the man who

planned every aspect of his life to protect his family.
Now he needed help getting in and out of cars, transferring
from his wheelchair, accessing ramps, and feared falls due to
missing signals from his spine to make his muscles work.

When Covid added another layer of confinement and seclusion,
something beautiful happened. Our limited lives became
the norm worldwide. We were like everyone else:
fearful, brave, confused. No one could travel,

everyone was stuck at home and we opened ourselves
to the microcosm of our world: our yard, our house, each room,
the windows, the inner workings of our hearts, the deep soul of
loss, the decades-long marriage that adapted in order to heal.

Speaking to Lake Superior Elders

It is the lake that I long for
and yet these rocks,

elders of the earth,
are what hold me here.

Once molten mountains,
they are now slabs

ground down by glacial ice
left here after the melt of time.

Now the rim of the cup
of this beautiful lake,

these slabs send heat into my back
as I lie in the sun, listening

to the push and pull of waves,
eyes shut as I picture them rolling in:

white ruffled edges against the dark and deep blue,
reaching their mark, then digging down,

scooping stones in the rhythm of earth and moon,
back and forth, in and out,

the breath of the lake,
the body of the lake inhaling, exhaling

until the rock itself and
the skins of the smaller stones below

are worn smooth as they rock
back and forth from the wear of daily life.

Ancient ones, what do you know
that you haven't yet told me?

Let Me Tell You About Our Yard

We never wanted yardwork in any house we lived in
and chose postage-stamp sized yards for ease in care.
This time we became open to a bigger yard with the plan
that we would hire help for yardwork and shoveling snow.

Our hearts opened when we found a home with nearly
an acre of land. A third of it is the front yard: a hill which
holds birch, several pine trees, an ironwood, and a simple
garden for the everchanging colors of perennials and annuals.

The backyard is flat and wide open, bordered with aging pines—
trunks covered in vines; a few ash trees; and room for growing
vegetables. The lawn, if I can call it that, is a combination of grass,
clover, wild strawberries, plantain, and, yes, creeping charley.

I love it all, especially knowing the plantain is full of calcium
and minerals; with a forest in back, there are innumerable
clusters of bunnies in the yard that would eagerly eat my hostas,
lilies, and flowers if not for the plantain. There are more varieties

of bees, moths, butterflies, and dragonflies than I have ever seen.
Insects abound and birds don't need to be fed anything extra in the
summer. The final third is the forest that flanks our backyard with
trees: evergreen, deciduous, and young saplings. Our home needed

to be one-level living but we scored a hotel, cabin, and retreat
center. Already in place were a fire pit, posts for volleyball, croquet
and badminton sets, and horseshoes. There is room for overnight
guests, and space to host large gatherings—everything we would

need to welcome family and bring people to us. Sitting by the fire
at night feels like the North Shore minus Lake Superior; a loss
since travel these days is harder. Although we were sad leaving our
last home, we are filled with love after finding such a paradise.

Sending Signals

There's the bunny sitting,
poised on the path
alongside the garden,
one paw pressed forward, resting
on the edging stone, eyes focused.

Every cell the bunny can muster
is sending signals to the nearby bunny,
but the stone garden bunny is mute,
can't see, can't receive, doesn't notice.

Close and in View

I am at the window
and they are back:
chickadees, robins, wrens
& goldfinches. The cardinal couple
flies onto an arborvitae branch,
hopping up close and in view,
jutting their heads out,
tipping their heads back.
He meets his mate
eye to eye, sometimes
one eye also on me
in the window.
Their bodies are cupped close
on their perches
softly saying
Isn't she beautiful.
Isn't he handsome.

April Courtship

Only a tinge of green
dapples tree branches
and undergrowth
visible in the woods

when two bunnies appear,
poised in an opening
of saplings, one on the left,
one on the right,

face to face, both
hunched down, gazing
eye to eye, five feet apart
when the male leans in and rises

bursting into a run, heading
for the female, who springs
into the air, a single hop
nearly three feet high.

Both rabbits flip their bodies
around, each taking turns
as the runner and jumper,
one darting, one leaping.

Later they come closer into the yard
just feet away from me
and begin the ritual again,
showing me the way to
celebrate life with a dance.

In Plain Sight

for Henry

A fox spotted by a neighbor gave me hope for a chance
to see one this winter. I have scoured our yard and
half-acre woods for signs, searching, with no luck.

What I really want is for Henry to see the fox,
or for the fox to spend a whole day in our yard
with chance of proof in pictures because

Henry loves foxes, wears his fox pants with regularity.
He could use a visit from a love, since Covid has
taken him from things that make his young life feel alive.

Foxes are the masters of camouflage, adept at blending in,
disappearing in plain sight, but in winter I thought
it would be easy to find him, red against white snow.

What we need now is the spiritual fox, an invisible
but available creature to walk us out of misery
and take us into the forest of fresh air.

Mouse Highway

I enter the bedroom in late morning
not knowing in his dream last night
Rod could walk again. He has walking
dreams that tint a new day gray.

He is silent in his wheelchair,
fixated on the western window.
I ask what he sees. *A mouse highway,*
he says. *Show me,* I say as I zero in on

a lush thicket of mature bushes, shrubs,
and meandering leafy vines that weave
to form a screen between the houses.
He points out the clutter of fallen pinecones,

boughs, and uneven undergrowth—a rollercoaster
terrain for a mouse—then the metal top rail
above the chain-link fence and the muddle below.
A mouse appears and easily walks the rail,

does not have to plow through or tunnel
under the debris below. Soon we observe
mice accessing the highway by climbing trunks
and vines to zoom along unencumbered.

It is the path of least resistance that Rod knows,
all barriers to his old life, and when he dreams
happy, then wakes to a wheelchair—waiting,
his sigh falls deeper and goes where it goes.

Sentries and One Wren

Eight blue jays swoop in and land at equal heights
in the pine trees that line the perimeter of our yard:
sentries standing guard overlooking the landscape.

I pause a moment when one more jay sweeps in,
landing on top of the post holding a birdhouse
where a wren has been diligently working on the nest.

The sentries watch the single jay as it hunches down,
its wings hanging low at its side. Alarm runs
up my spine when I remember jays steal eggs.

I grab a stepstool and dart toward the wren house
just as the jay lands on the perch. I shoo him away
with a swipe of my hand, then peek inside.

All I see is carefully arranged sticks with no view
of the inner basin of the nest. I lean closer and the wren
zips out straight at my forehead, lifting the hair

on the top of my head, landing in a pine tree, rousted
in an angry chatter. My heart aches for her sense of danger,
her fear of me: the sentry who was truly trying to protect.

Remembering a Hike in the Mountains
with My Norwegian Relatives

The bear of the past lumbers along
as we hike the mountains in Förde,

stopping like us, to feed along the way.
The women point out berries in bushes

and those nested in low-lying plants
easily missed, jeweled offerings known

to me now since they are placed
on the dinner table before me each night.

❖

The day I arrived, we sat down to a
beautifully laid out meal of steelhead trout

baked whole, with potatoes and carrots,
butter melting, steam rising, the flesh of

the drizzled fish moist and succulent,
candles lit, lighting low, smiles all around.

The antique clock in the kitchen chimes
at 7:00 and again at half past. I revel

in its charm, while my relatives, alarmed,
say that the clock hasn't chimed in years.

*Janet, I think your Norwegian ancestors
are welcoming you back,* cousin Arne says.

❖

The heavy mist keeps us and the
lumbering bear from seeing what lies ahead

as we climb higher or head back down
along the streams in the valley below.

Years later I learn the clock never chimed again.

That illusive old bear senses stories untold,
holds them, some to forever remain unknown.

Unexpected Blessing

I see a wild turkey poised in our backyard.
I watch the turkey fly up onto the porch overhang,
strut to the rooftop and walk the complete spine of the roof,
one eye on me as she surveys the four directions.

Inside the house, my husband pauses. Burdened by
his illness, he takes a deep breath, then lifts himself
off the bed using only his arms to transfer to his wheelchair,
grateful for his grit and upper body strength.

I am the witness of the turkey's beauty, stature,
and diligent duty. I accept it as only one thing:
a good omen that I will hold onto for both of us,
hope now and in the future as we navigate our lives together.

Resurrection

The opossum prevails
as she makes her way all around
the empty screened-in porch,
paws pressing prints into the relentless snow,
her pink snout lifted as she sniffs up and away
showing her little overbite,
baring teeth she doesn't intend to use.

She heads out of sight, a private crusade
of her own making, only later to be found by
a surprised home inspector who reports her dead
in the window well and recommends
the owner buy cheap window well covers
to avoid other unintended deaths.

Alarmed, the homeowner rushes out to find the body
to gather it up for a proper burial, but it is gone,
no trace, no rolled-away stone, just gone.

The owner smiles at the emptiness, knowing
she did what opossums do. Drama queen
of the animal world—she rolled over, played dead,
(the death scent rising to the nose of the inspector)—
a perfect performance. Then she rose up
and wandered on into the woods.

Legacy

for Brooks

We are looking at a porcelain plate
with three timber wolves painted on it.
The moon is full and the wolves
are crossing a snowbank along the river.
Guess which wolf I like the best, Nana.
There are two prominent wolves in the foreground
leading the way, but Brooks chooses the wolf standing
in the background to the right of the pine tree.
There is a stream of breath coming out of the wolf's mouth.
I used to think the wolf was smoking a cigarette,
Brooks says, with a smile, and we both laugh.
I look at all three wolves in the picture
and see that the one he chose is the only one
that stands eye to eye looking directly at him,
showing determination, power, and the vitality of breath.

The Lesson

I first saw the doe, high on the ledge,
then two fawns
as they stepped out
past their mother
to small arms of
land angled downward
against the surrounding eroding sand.

I wondered why the doe
let them roam beyond her,
why she didn't try to corral them back to safety
where they would be hidden in the trees,
less likely to lose footing in a landslide.
We do that, take our young into our hearts.
Then, there they are, running ahead
to a world that calls to them
in ways we don't understand.

Shades of Blue

When I learned Arne died,
I knew it would be hard for Mom to hear.
Her beloved younger cousin from Norway
had passed before her. I called her and gazed
out the window as I waited for her to answer.
Sadness squeezed the depth and strength
from my voice as I told her. She was silent.
Then through my window to the backyard
I saw three bluebirds flying from one low-lying branch
to another—small, round, and rosy-breasted.
I had waited a lifetime to see a bluebird.
They look grey until they fly, Mom,
then they burst into a brilliant blue.

That's the way they are, she answered.
I glanced down at a nearby picture
of Mom, Dad, and Arne taken years ago.
My first bluebirds: one for each of them.
Arne and Dad both gone, but at least
Mom is still here, I think, delighted that there are
three bluebirds now present in my yard. So much beauty
and my mother's favorite color to savor.
Three weeks later, the bluebirds are still here
when I learn my mother has passed
into the deep blue of their wings in flight.

To Make My Thoughts a Map

In the lowlands now, I hear the sound
of a bird hidden in the rushes, camouflaged,
reverberating a call I can't quite identify,
quiet at first, then intensified
as the long, lean bird emerges from the reeds.

I am struck by his stature, legs long, red clay body feathers,
cream-colored neck, and bright red crown.
Sandhill crane, I whisper.

He passes me and heads up a hill, calling.
I remember the sandhill cranes who gather every year
at Carver and hold them in my thoughts.
Go there, find them, I think, as if thoughts could be a map.
When he lifts up with his wings spread wide and heads north,
I think, *That's right, that's right, turn west soon.*
They will be there in the fields calling for you.

Squirrels: A Day Well Spent

I completely ignored them all summer,
their common gray blending into bark
did not compete with cardinal red,
the indigo magic of the bluebird, orange and black
of the oriole, the gilded goldfinch, or even
the drably dressed tiny wren who can belt out
an aria that trills the air, makes all things pause.

An early snow changed things. I saw their gray coats
lush against the white snow, their busyness for what is:
organized preparedness. Their frenetic movements are
a ballroom dance covering every square inch of the stage,
noting every available resource for daily living, all while
keeping past and future in mind as they store their caches today.

A friend joked that every time she saw a squirrel
it had a bunch of leaves in its mouth, and soon, she believed,
her yard would be raked. Maybe so, but for certain the squirrel's
nest will be plush and it will sleep in the bough of a day well spent.

Wedding Anniversary 2020

The occasion of our anniversary finds us bereft
of our usual affections, longings, memories of
those first days, years, hopes we had for each day.
I look out a window to the backyard, see the
outline of a large owl perched on a pine branch
at the edge of the woods. Fingers of fine branches from
neighboring trees don't reach or hide the stature of
the great horned owl that looks my way, then turns
her head to reveal her magnificent feather-tufted horns.

I rush to our bedroom, pull back the drapes to show Rod.
He scans the woods but can't see her from this angle.
I grab the handles on his wheelchair and push him,
speeding down the hall to a better window, hoping he will
get a clear view before she flies away. *Oh, yeah, that's a
great horned alright,* he says as we stare at her in silence.
After we retire for the night, we hear two owls calling
one to the other, first the female and then the male,
the female, then the male, beautiful and haunting.

Moon or Star

Let me go back to the two fawns—
did I tell you how my heart raced?
How rare it is to see
their auburn-caramel fur
delicately smattered with white
as if their mother's love
kissed them again and again
leaving a moon or star,
a map to find each other,
so neither one
would ever be lost to the other.

Good News

I should have noticed, should have received
all of the messages coming my way:
the turkey blessing our home;
the once empty hummingbird feeder
welcoming an adorable hummer all so
we could catch a glimpse of her mysterious
iridescence as she sipped and relished the nectar;
the two wren couples who took turns,
one after the other, raising their young
in the birdhouse I inherited from my mom.
All the birds that sang to me
wherever I was in the yard,
the tomato plants placed in the
only spot we had, not the best light
or soil, yet now, in early July are
nearly as tall as I am and attracting the most
beautiful golden dragonflies I have ever seen.
Oh, and the darling deer who couldn't resist
eating my best hostas and lilies for sustenance
after she gave birth to her fawn in our forest.
I should have known it could only be good news:
The cancer is still disappearing, the doctor said,
His immune system is working, making it go away.

Meteor Shower

Evening begins with all of us together,
like children sequestered in the
neighborhood fort at the edge of the woods,

yet we are no longer children,
there are no woods, only open sky as we lie
on an outcrop of rock at the edge of Lake Superior,

looking up, laughing, firing one joke
after another, each one trying to outdo the other
when nature pulls a fast one and outdoes us all,

first with one shooting star, then another
and another, until we lose count and succumb.
We know they aren't shooting stars,

but caught in the memory of ourselves as children,
that's what we call them tonight. Older now,
we also know time does not actually exist,

but the movement of a meteor does,
and moments do, like the frame-by-frame
stills of the life of a child rising, arcing,

burning bright, then disappearing
into the darkness. And we are
mesmerized by the wild uprising,

the falling of fire created by the cosmos,
the pull of gravity bringing us closer to each other,
closer to those ever-present and disappearing stars.

Nesters

A mallard couple showed up yesterday,
casing out the backyard, poking around
along the deck and sideyard woods
as if hunting for a nesting place.
I deemed it unlikely they would follow through, though.

Today, I rise early and there they are,
staring right into the front picture window.
The male, protective, eyes looking squarely at me;
the female, wary, sneaking a sideways glance
through squinted eyes; both freezing a bit before
they waddle away along the edging plants
scouting a prime location to put down roots.

New to the neighborhood, I remember the small pond
tucked down in a hollow below a row of houses.
It would be a quick beeline cutting through
a couple of yards, then a jaunt down the hill,
and voilá, water for the ducklings! Married
for decades now, it would be nice to have another
devoted couple join us for the summer.

Recognition

When I hear a wren calling from the yard
and I am inside the house, I picture it,
either in the eastern pine or the southern birch.
The same with robins, chickadees, bluebirds, cardinals,
blue jays, crows, flickers, and the downys.
Yesterday a new sound drew me to the window,
an ominous high-pitched resonance
almost prehistoric, and there they were:
two pileated woodpeckers, wild-topped, bright red heads,
black bodies, with white stripes around the face,
the male having an extra red cheek-stripe.
Their presence exuded perseverance, strength, and determination.
Stunningly beautiful, they stayed in the trees for hours.
Today the sound of three crows cawing
breaks the air like the snap of a leather strap
and brings me to my feet to witness the commotion.
All three fates: past, present, and future
careening in and around a towering pine,
until each bird veers off—up, out, and away.

Angel Deer

I gasped when I came upon her,
a tawny beauty curled into herself,

front legs tucked under her body,
her long neck angled back, head nestled

under her left thigh as if to wrap herself
into the shawl of her body. Touching

and sweet at first, a shiver ran through me
when I saw the stillness of her eye, glazed over

and open wide. The wing of her ear
cupped like a flower petal invited a wish

that I could have whispered into it—
I wish I could have saved you.

Serene Within

Heron swoops in and lands on a limestone slab
jutting out from the shoreline along the river.
Two dragonflies sweep the air surrounding
heron's head, separate at first, then whirl around
to become linked in their mating ritual.

The passion displayed calls to me:
stand tall for the world, remain serene within.
Make love, make love, fly and buzz, drink in air,
sing all the colors found within the dragon's wing.

My Dream

A man appears, tall and thin.
He motions for me to follow
as he begins to run along
a red clay path that carves its way
through a tropical forest.
It is sweltering, and I think,
I am not a runner. I can't run in this heat.
I am not breathless or encumbered.
I welcome the scooped-out trail,
the red clay, hard beneath my feet,
the banked turns I master.

I stay with the leader, evolving,
shifting my energy and hugging
the path now, lower, closer to the
ground, and then the man is gone.
Power courses through my blood.
A boreal forest surrounds me now.
I am filled with bliss. This is no mistake,
or lucky break—this is my place, the real me.

I look down and my feet are paws.
I am running on all fours, my tongue
hanging out, and behind me, the puff
of my beautiful tail. I am fur and fury.
In the distance, I hear the howl of a wolf.
The lone and lonely wolf, it seems,
remembering childhood tales of wolves.
Not true, I feel in my bones as I run.
The howl rings out again and I hear both
the sound and translation: *Not Alone.*
The wolf calls out again, and then
a cacophony of wolves all calling out,
Not alone, not alone, not alone.

The Beloved

Don't be saddened by the fate of the ash.
It is yet to be determined. Grandfather ash holds court
near the neighboring woods, commands respect

with his wide-reaching arms heralding up
toward heaven, feeding, shading, and comforting
every living creature in his presence.

The tree was slated to be taken down this winter.
On the scheduled day we woke to subzero weather
that wasn't safe for the workers to come.

A sad morning grew into a measure of hope,
the possibility for all things, the potential of at least
one more spring and summer with the beloved.

Rosie

I wondered if I would ever find a dog.
Then there she was, Rosie, the golden-eyed
scruffy terrier with a pink nose. Her picture
listed on Golden Valley's humane society website.
So many dogs with tender histories are afraid of people
(often men). Some cower at loud noises.
Angst-ridden ones from puppy mills sometimes
don't even know how to be dogs. Some sites specify,
This one will never work out with a wheelchair. Too skittish.
When I saw Rosie's picture, I was first in line before they opened.
She was mine before I even held her.

At home, she ran straight to Rod in his wheelchair,
wagged her tail, put her paws on his lap and licked his hands.
Rosie, a Mississippi transplant, was a keeper. Rod spoke to her
in a southern accent to make her feel at home
and burst into song with little ditties: *How much is that Rosie,*
in the window? The one with the little pink nose.

When Brooks and Henry came to see her,
they were overwhelmed by Rosie's hugs and kisses.
Look at her cream-colored body with the golden fur on top—
a perfectly roasted marshmallow, Henry laughed.
And, look, she has gold eye-liner around her eyes, added Brooks.
Oh Nana! She is so friendly. She can fit in any family.

In the backyard, she scanned the woods and the lawn,
surveyed the house and walked toward the backdoor.
She looked up at me with her turned-down mouth.
In her eyes I saw: *I hit the jackpot.* The feeling was mutual.

Fortune

What about twenty-four goldfinches filling the branches
of a perfectly shaped tree in the middle of a meadow?
A tree washed in gold, all of the finches singing,
their golden bodies painting the tree
with the brushstrokes of their feathers.

Without warning all twenty-four lift up,
leave the tree, arch over the pathway
where I am standing, and land in a sister tree,
glorify it, bless it in the name of wind, water, and wealth.
All that gold changing hands, offered up to anyone
lucky enough to witness.

Special Thanks

I would like to thank my family for their support of my writing. My wonderful husband Rod is often my first reader and sees my work in its roughest form. I can trust his honesty and admire his courage when he tells me my writing needs revision. My son Anton and his wife Emily read several of my poems and offered encouragement as I developed this book. My daughter Anna and her husband Oskar gave kind support from afar since they lived in Sweden during this book's writing. My brothers Rick, David, Daniel, and Steve are kind and supportive of everything I do and always show interest in my poems.

I want to extend a very special heartfelt thank-you to my two grandsons, Brooks and Henry, who not only love the two poems in the book that are dedicated to them but were enthusiastic about my writing process as well. They asked questions about the poems and understood metaphor and depth in poetry. When I first shared Henry's poem with the boys, thirteen-year-old Brooks said, *Wow, Nana, that is really deep. It means so many things.* Henry was so excited about my poems and the book that he asked his third-grade teacher if I could come to school to discuss the writing process and how to get a book published.

Successful writers do not write in isolation. I have been a member of two poetry groups for decades, and I would like to thank these strong, brave women for their writing, creativity, thoughtful editing, and their *joie de vivre*. I cherish all of them for their individual journeys that have led to their contributions to the world of poetry. There are many times when I have been in a meeting or become aware of some chilling aspect of life, and I wonder, *Where are the poets? We need a poet here to bring depth and understanding to this situation.* It is then that I am relieved to once again meet with them: Teresa Boyer, Jacey Choy, Kirsten Dierking,

Ann Iverson, Rita Moe, Nancy Walden, Kathy Weihe, Liz Weir, and Tracy Youngblom—are all wonderful writers. I am honored and grateful to the poets who wrote kind words on the back of my book; Deborah Keenan, a generous and longtime mentor of mine and to at least half of the Minnesota poets; Michael Kleber-Diggs, who was awarded Milkweed Editions' Max Ritvo Poetry Prize; and Ann Iverson, author of several books, a longtime friend and artist.

A very special thanks to friend Rita Moe for her detailed and careful editing of this book.

I feel so much gratitude to my childhood friend and artist, Maarja Roth, whom I have known since fifth grade. I love the stunningly beautiful cover art she created for *A Map to Find Each Other*.

Finally, many thanks to the Loppet Ski Club members; if it weren't for our year-round activities, I wouldn't have had as much fun getting outside to ski, bicycle, and hike and, in the process, discover so many animals. Companionship was fun, especially with Susan Schultz, who was with me when I saw the deer and fawns, the sandhill crane, and the goldfinches.

About the Author

Janet Jerve's lifetime work has been as an educator: a teacher, trainer, and writer of educational materials. She has worked with all ages: infants and parents, grade school children, and adults in public schools and various non-profit settings. The overall focus of her work was to provide learning experiences that supported and empowered all her students, with a special interest in helping underserved learners and their parents.

After taking classes at the Loft Literary Center in 1985, Janet started writing poetry and was introduced to the vibrant and engaging poetry community in Minnesota, one of the most supportive in the country. Over the years, she joined many writing groups and began to teach poetry in her classrooms. She learned that many children who struggled with reading and writing thrived writing poetry. It opened them up to the world of writing; they found their voices in their work and became better readers, too.

Her poems have appeared in literary journals, including *Poetry East, Water~Stone Review, Great River Review, Lake Effect, Hurricane Alice,* and *Emprise Review.* Her work has been included in anthologies: *A Ghost at Heart's Edge,* published by North Atlantic Books; *Beloved on the Earth, The Heart of All That Is,* and *Amethyst and Agate: Poems of Lake Superior,* all anthologies published by Holy Cow! Press. Her first book of poetry, *Excavation,* was published in 2013 by North Star Press.

Janet loves art and knitting and enjoys a variety of outdoor activities. She teaches Nordic skiing to adults for the Loppet Ski Club at Wirth Park in Minneapolis. She lives in Bloomington with her husband Rod and dog Rosie.

www.ingramcontent.com/pod-product-compliance
Lightning Source LLC
Chambersburg PA
CBHW071359090426
42738CB00012B/3167